Original title:
Brambleberry Rhymes

Copyright © 2025 Creative Arts Management OÜ
All rights reserved.

Author: Samuel Kensington
ISBN HARDBACK: 978-1-80567-340-8
ISBN PAPERBACK: 978-1-80567-639-3

Echoes in the Woodland Choir

In the woods where the bushes giggle,
Squirrels dance and rabbits wiggle.
A crow caws, it's quite absurd,
Joining in with the chattering herd.

A fox with a hat and a glowing tail,
Tells jokes to the deer, they never fail.
The owls hoot a comical tune,
As frogs croak in a leafy commune.

Festivities of the Murmuring Roots

Underneath where the roots all meld,
The critters gather, their laughter swelled.
A mole with a top hat settles down,
As the rabbits wear glasses and get quite clown.

The ants serve snacks in stylish stacks,
While the hedgehogs play cards, avoiding cracks.
A beetle spins tales from days of yore,
And the badgers applaud, always wanting more.

Fables of the Berry-Laden Banks

By the river where the berries grow,
A jubilant turtle steals the show.
With blueberries stuck to its shell,
It wobbles around, under a sweet spell.

The ducks quack in rhythm, quite the jam,
As a raccoon sneaks off with a strawberry slam.
A frog in a cape gives a jumping cheer,
While bear in the background hums with a beer.

Lament of the Thorny Fray

In the thicket where thorns like to fight,
A porcupine sports armor, what a sight!
With a grin and a shrug, it declares,
'These prickly foes can't bother my hairs!'

A chattering magpie swoops down to tease,
While the hedgehogs roll back, such antics please.
Though brambles may sting and thorns may pry,
These silly squabbles are never awry.

Tasting Sunlight and Shadows

Sunlight spills like jam on toast,
Shadows dance a silly boast.
In fields where daisies poke their heads,
We giggle where the mischief spreads.

Butterflies in polka dots,
Wear funny hats, they tie their knots.
We chase a squirrel with acorn dreams,
Riding on a river of silly streams.

In the Arms of Nature's Wild

A raccoon wears a top hat proud,
While singing tunes both loud and loud.
The trees break out in laughter free,
As nature winks at you and me.

With squirrel friends who juggle nuts,
They plan a party, dress in cuts.
A picnic feast on leafy grounds,
With laughter echoing all around.

Berrying by the Stream

Wading in a berry patch,
Squeaky shoes and laughter match.
The berries giggle, red and sweet,
As we gather them with dancing feet.

A frog joins in, a jolly croak,
He tells bad jokes that make us choke.
With every splash, a joyful cheer,
Nature's whimsy drawing near.

Gathering in the Tangled Brush

In tangles where the wild things play,
We find a treasure every day.
A hedgehog wears a tiny hat,
And rolls around like quite the brat.

A charming rabbit runs amok,
Dodging all the silly luck.
We gather stories, leaf and sprout,
In nature's giggle, there's no doubt.

Thorns and Melodies

In the thicket where thorns delight,
A squirrel sings with all his might.
He dances on branches, full of glee,
While bees buzz tunes in harmony.

The fox joins in, with a wink and a grin,
Crafting funny tales, letting laughter begin.
A rabbit hops, oh what a sight,
Chasing his shadow, with sheer delight.

The Secret Grove's Lullaby

In a grove where secrets play,
Owls hoot jokes at the end of the day.
The moonlight giggles, twinkling bright,
As fireflies dance, a shimmering flight.

A raccoon croons, a sleepy tune,
While crickets laugh underneath the moon.
With every note, dreams are spun,
In the secret grove, where funny's begun.

Sweetness in the Thicket

In the thicket where berries grow,
A chubby bear comes on the show.
With sticky paws, he starts to hum,
And little critters join in the fun.

A hedgehog rolls, with laughter accrued,
Bouncing along, in a berry mood.
Sweetness drips from their joyful spree,
In the thicket where giggles run free.

Echoes of Twisted Vines

Amidst the vines that twist and twirl,
A merry lizard starts to whirl.
With every flick of his colorful tail,
The forest echoes with a laughing gale.

A chattering parrot lends its voice,
While rabbits jump, oh what a choice!
In every corner, there's joy to find,
In the echoes of those twisted vines.

Lanterns of the Darkening Woods

In the woods where shadows play,
Lanterns wink, they dance away.
Squirrels gossip, owls just stare,
While fireflies buzz without a care.

A raccoon tiptoes, steals a snack,
Wearing a mask, it's on the attack!
The trees shake hands, they creak and groan,
As night descends, they're not alone.

The Flavor of Forgotten Paths

On paths where lost socks end their quest,
We munch on leaves, oh, what a jest!
Mushrooms giggle, they're quite the crowd,
Their funky hats worn oh so proud.

The breeze brings scents of pickle pie,
We munch and laugh, oh my, oh my!
With every step, a new delight,
As flavors whirl beneath the light.

Curry of the Sun and Shade

In pots of gold beneath the sun,
Curry simmers, oh, what fun!
Spices twirl in flavorful glee,
While beans start dancing, wild and free.

Through sunny spots and shadows deep,
The taste of laughter, we shall keep.
Garlic whispers, not too loud,
Join the feast, let's gather a crowd!

Mystic Gardens in Twilight

In gardens where the odd things grow,
Awkward creatures put on a show.
A honeybee in a top hat sips,
While dancing snails do funny flips.

The moonlight spills like silly soap,
Lighting up the path of hope.
With giggles echoing through the night,
In mystic gardens, all feels right.

Verses Woven in the Underbrush

In a thicket of laughter, the critters convene,
Berries bouncing about, like a fruity machine.
Squirrels dressed silly, with hats made of leaves,
Sharing their secrets, if only one believes.

Under the bushes, where giggles abound,
A raccoon with rhythm, the funniest sound.
With each little dance, they began a parade,
Making a ruckus, not one was afraid.

The Song of the Ripening Fields

In fields full of giggles, the vegetables sing,
With carrots in chorus, and birds on the wing.
Cabbages chuckling, in a leafy delight,
They hold a grand concert every soft night.

The beans all are dancing, twirling in rows,
While potatoes do prance, in their funny clothes.
Laughter in the breeze, a sweet, playful cheer,
As the moonlight chuckles, saying, 'I'm here!'

Whimsical Weavings in the Bramble

Once in a meadow, where shadows align,
A hedgehog wore glasses, claiming, 'I'm fine!'
With berries like jewels, so bright on his back,
He strutted and fretted, in tactical black.

The fox joined the fun, in a costume so sly,
Dressed up like a berry, beneath a bright sky.
They played hide and seek, under archways of green,
Chasing giggles and sighs, a delightful scene.

Memories of a Forgotten Harvest

Once upon a crew, of quirky old plants,
With tomatoes that tangoed, and melons in pants.
Corn cob with a mustache, said, 'I'll lead the way!'
Forgetting their harvest, they'd dance every day.

The pumpkins were waltzing, a sight to behold,
While squash snickered softly, their stories retold.
In the heart of the garden, such madness unfurled,
As laughter took root, in this jolly old world.

Sunlit Thorns and Velvet Dreams

In the garden, thorns do sway,
Jokes and jests in the light of day.
Velvet leaves with a cheeky grin,
Tickling toes as we dive in.

Bumblebees buzz in a dance so sweet,
While ants march on with their tiny feet.
Giggles hidden in the bushy green,
Nature's laughter, rarely seen.

A squirrel slips on a berry pie,
Flapping its paws as it tries to fly.
Sunlit thorns, a ticklish game,
Nature's mischief, never the same.

Under the sun, our laughter spills,
Amongst the blooms and hilltop thrills.
Nature's quirks, a playful scheme,
In this world of velvet dreams.

Harvest Moon's Sweet Caress

The moon hangs low, a glowing tease,
With ripe delights carried on the breeze.
Laughter echoes from the fields at night,
As shadows play in the silver light.

A raccoon juggles apples with flair,
While owls hoot, offering a scare.
Under the harvest, secrets fold,
Tales of jest, in stories told.

The night is wild with playful haste,
A dance of berries, none to waste.
Each bite whispers a curious joke,
A secret shared in the moon's soft cloak.

Underneath the harvest's glow,
Frolicsome antics put on a show.
With every chuckle that fills the air,
The moon's sweet caress, without a care.

Notes from the Wild Berry Grove

In the grove where the wild things grow,
Laughter echoes, a playful flow.
Berries tumble with a giggly spree,
Whispering secrets on rustling leaves.

A fox with flair, holds a berry bash,
While rabbits hop, making quite the splash.
Every berry has a tale, you see,
Of silly dances and jubilee.

With strawberries sharing tales of woe,
And blueberries wearing hats in a row.
Nature's symphony, a giddy tune,
Played under the glow of a rosy moon.

In this grove, the fun is grand,
Brambling joy, hand in hand.
Each berry ripe with a story twined,
Forever etched in nature's mind.

The Language of Hidden Fruits

In the hush of leaves, a whisper's found,
Secrets hiding all around.
Pineapple crowns and banana grins,
Speak of mischief the moment begins.

Cherries giggle in the summer sun,
Poking fun, oh what a run!
Grapevines twist, sharing silly jests,
While lemons frown, wearing their vests.

With every bite, a chuckle grows,
A fruity tale that everybody knows.
Among the vines, the humor's ripe,
Jokes exchanged, like secret type.

Beneath the surface, fruits conspire,
With laughter's spark, they never tire.
In every orchard, a chuckle bursts,
In this sweet dance of hidden fruits.

The Patchwork of Nature's Heart

In the garden, flowers caper,
Wobbling about like silly paper.
Bees wear hats, quite out of style,
While butterflies dance, making us smile.

A tomato sings a jaunty tune,
While carrots watch beneath the moon.
Giggling veggies, what a sight,
Nature's humor, pure delight!

The sun threw a party; shadows came,
Everyone danced, forgetting their name.
The earth chuckled, feet in the dirt,
Even the weeds wore a lively skirt.

Laughter ripples through the air,
As squirrels juggle seeds with flair.
In this patchwork, all things play,
Nature's heart, in vibrant array.

Clandestine Harvest Moon

Under the cloak of twilight's glow,
The moon whispers secrets we don't know.
Berries giggle, high in the trees,
While raccoons throw parties, munching on peas.

Frogs in tuxedos croak out a jam,
With crickets playing backup, oh what a slam!
A hidden dance where the shadows twirl,
Nature's mischief, in a whimsical whirl.

A scarecrow cheers with arms in the air,
Declaring victory, amidst the fair.
His corncob pipe puffs out sweet smoke,
While pumpkins snicker; it's all a joke!

The moon, a trickster, shines and hides,
While critters gossip on wild rides.
Under its watch, the laughter blooms,
A harvest full of giggles and tunes.

Roaming Through Briar's Care

Through thickets thick, we laugh and roam,
In tangled paths, we find our home.
A bushy cat with a winking eye,
Offers us berries as we pass by.

Brambles weave stories, none too clear,
They giggle and rustle, drawing us near.
A hedgehog whispers, 'Stay out of trouble!'
As we bounce through the thorns, bursting with bubble.

Dancing shadows flicker like sprites,
As we chase daylight, embracing the nights.
In this wild embrace of green and gray,
Every briar's tale leads us astray.

A silly snail rides on a leaf,
While laughter sings, chasing off grief.
Wandering free in briar's charms,
We find our joy within nature's arms.

Pies and Poetry in the Glen

In the glen where laughter stirs,
Pies are baking, scented with spurs.
Cheery folks gather, forks in hand,
Sharing rhymes and a berry band.

Each slice served with a giggly rhyme,
Tickles our hearts, feels sublime.
A peachy pie whispers secrets sweet,
While crusty jokes dance on our feet.

The oven hums a melodic tune,
As pastries puff beneath the moon.
A cherry tumbles, rolling about,
Spreading joy, never a doubt!

In this merry place, tales are spun,
Of apples, laughter, and lots of fun.
With every bite, our spirits fly,
In the glen, where dreams never die.

The Return to the Tangled Wild

In the thicket where critters play,
A squirrel danced in a wobbly way,
He tripped on a vine, oh what a sight,
As the bushes all giggled in sheer delight.

A rabbit with socks, what a wild scene,
Hopped on a log, like a dancing machine,
He slipped on a leaf, with a thud and a thwack,
And we all burst out laughing, none holding back.

With brambles that whispered their cheeky tales,
Of hedgehogs planning their berry-filled trails,
A fox in a hat, strutting with flair,
Who painted his whiskers, now, that's quite rare!

So let's roam the wild, with giggles galore,
With berry-stained fingers, we'll laugh and explore,
In the tangled chaos, oh what a thrill,
Join the dance of the wild, if you're ever so still.

Journey Through a Berry Sanctuary

In the heart of the field, where the berries are bright,
A turtle in sneakers took off in delight,
With a bounce and a roll, he claimed the best prize,
While a crow cawed a tune that was mildly unwise.

We met a chubby hedgehog, named Ned,
He wore a small crown on his fuzzy head,
As he governed the patch, with laughter and cheer,
With a berry pie formula, that was perfectly clear.

An owl with a monocle perched on a tree,
Said, "Who's in charge? You, or are you not free?"
With a wink and a hoot, he flew round and round,
Tracing mazes of giggles, with joy unbound.

As we tasted the sweetness, we fell in a jam,
With sticky fingers and faces, oh what a slam!
Yet, we danced in the splendor, no worries in sight,
In our berry-filled haven, everything felt right.

Nectar Splashes of the Heart

In a garden of laughter, where the flowers all cheer,
A bee in a bowtie buzzed round with a leer,
She slipped on a petal, took quite a fine dive,
And landed in nectar, oh how she did thrive!

A butterfly visited, wearing glasses so cool,
She flitted and fluttered, but played the fool,
With a gust of a breeze, her specs flew away,
While she danced with the daisies, much to her dismay.

In this nectar oasis, mischief is grand,
A raccoon in overalls raised up his hand,
He juggled ripe peaches with a grin ear to ear,
Then dropped them all, shouting, "Let's keep it near!"

But with laughter that echoed, we found all our cheer,
In the splashes of nectar, we held nothing dear,
With friends all around, we relished the fun,
In a whimsical world, where joy had begun.

Twisted Vines of Memory

In the garden, laughter grows,
With tangled vines, all in rows.
A cat in a hat twirls and spins,
While mice throw a party, let the fun begin!

Those berries' whispers tell a tale,
Of a pickle wearing a vibrant veil.
Each twist recalls a silly sight,
As gnomes dance happily through the night.

In that patch where giggles bloom,
A squirrel with shades consumes his gloom.
Amidst the blossoms, joy's the theme,
In this garden of topsy-turvy dreams.

So join the jests under the sky,
With fruity antics that make you sigh.
From juicy tales and grapevine cheer,
We'll laugh and ponder, year after year.

Musings Among the Thorns

Beneath the brambles, thoughts take flight,
With prickers poking, it's quite the sight.
A hedgehog wears a tutu so bright,
While butterflies giggle in sheer delight.

Oh, thorns can scratch, yet they also sway,
Like bowls of jelly in a humorous play.
Ants march in step, forming a train,
While rabbits hop, dodging drops of rain.

With every twist, a chuckle grows,
As loopy loops seem to steal the show.
We'll weave our stories, tangled and free,
In this prickly patch of whimsy and glee.

So tread with care on this fun-filled ground,
Where laughter and mischief are always found.
Among the thorns, we'll dance and prance,
In the fiddlesticks of a silly romance.

The Lullaby of Rustic Fruits

Underneath the apple tree,
A chorus sings in harmony.
With each ripe fruit, a giggle flows,
As peaches wear their fuzzy clothes.

The cherries tell jokes, one by one,
While lemons chuckle, having fun.
A pear in a bowtie steals the scene,
As pickles wiggle, oh so green!

"Berry, berry good," the chorus hums,
As silly rhymes tap like little drums.
In this orchard, where craziness reigns,
Each fruit is bursting with playful gains.

So sway in the branches, partake in the night,
With laughter and joy that feels so right.
The lullaby of nature sings on cue,
In our fruity world of giggles anew.

A Tangle of Enchanted Verses

In the thicket, magic stirs,
With dancing weeds and chirping spurs.
A dandelion turns into a crown,
While tulips gossip, wearing a frown.

Each word a vine, every rhyme a twist,
With butterflies clutching their to-do list.
A dragonfly plays hopscotch on leaves,
While ladybugs giggle, ready to tease.

Through this playful maze of green,
The silliest sights one could ever glean.
With wobbly verse, we'll find our way,
In a muddle of fun, come what may!

So join the chant, let's frolic and sway,
In this enchanted world where we play.
Amidst the thorns, the laughter grows,
In our tangle of verses, joy overflows.

Whispers of Wild Thorns

In the patch where shadows play,
A squirrel sings at end of day.
With tiny bells that clink and chime,
He's lost the plot, but just in time.

The thorns all giggle, oh what fun,
As berries tumble, one by one.
A raspberry rolls, with quite the grace,
And smacks the hedgehog in the face!

A thrush pipes up with quirky lines,
About the fruit and mishaps fine.
While all around the wild things share,
Their tales of laughter, light as air.

And as the sun begins to fade,
The critters dance where shades cascade.
In thickets deep where giggles bloom,
The joys of wild thorns light the gloom.

The Dance of Juicy Shadows

In twilight's glow, the shadows prance,
With juicy tales that make you dance.
A blueberry rolls, it slips and trips,
    Causing giggles and berry quips.

A grape spins round with dizzy flair,
While cherries bounce without a care.
The rasp of thorns joins in the beat,
    As bumblebees tap tiny feet.

The fig performs a daring twirl,
    While wildflowers give a whirl.
Their laughter rings through leaves so green,
As fireflies twinkle, join the scene.

And in this dusk, pure joy abounds,
With fruity laughter, nature sounds.
A waltz of whimsy fills the air,
In shadows juicy, none can compare.

Thickets of Sweet Echoes

In thickets thick, where echoes dwell,
A clever fox spins tales to tell.
He juggles fruits with flair and charm,
While owls look on, their eyes alarmed.

Berry bushes rustle with glee,
As bunnies laugh at his wild spree.
The tart of plums and sweetness bright,
Bring bursts of joy in the soft light.

A good-natured vine slips in a twist,
And all join in, they can't resist.
They twirl and bounce, a leafy song,
In this thicket, nothing goes wrong.

So if you wander through this place,
Expect to see a funny face.
For in the woods, the echoes cheer,
Sweet tales of laughter fill your ear.

Fables in the Berry Patch

Once upon a time, they say,
In a patch where berries play.
A sneaky worm chose quite the fruit,
To call his home, oh isn't that cute?

A strawberry grinned, it spilled the beans,
On all the antics of these queens.
With thorns like crowns, they ruled the lot,
While raspberries plotted in a pot.

The wise old beetle, full of dreams,
Composed a tale, or so it seems.
With every nibble and juicy cheer,
The patch would laugh and draw you near.

In this patch where fables bloom,
Every giggle casts away gloom.
So join the fruits, both wild and sweet,
In this enchanted, berry treat.

Tangle of Dreaming Twigs

In a twisty tangle of twigs,
A squirrel wears socks, oh what a rig!
He dances around with berries galore,
While the owls in the tree just snore.

Marshmallow toes on a sunny day,
The rabbits surge forth in wild display.
With hiccuping hops, they leap quite high,
And the birds in the branches all sigh.

Hearts filled with giggles, laughter erupts,
As the fox pranks the deer, oh how he disrupts!
Frolicking creatures beneath the bright moon,
They all sing out loud, a merry tune.

Wobbly hedgehogs play tag with the breeze,
Bumbling along with the buzz of the bees.
In the tangle of twigs, mischief ignites,
A symphony's born on these carefree nights.

Sweet Shadows in the Forest

In the forest where shadows play,
A bear tells a joke in a silly way.
With berries stuck upon his hat,
He's off to find a lunch with a spat.

A chorus of giggles fills the glade,
As turtles shimmy, their coolness displayed.
The squirrels throw acorns; oh what a blast,
While raccoons play poker with coins they amassed.

Underneath the leaves, a whispering breeze,
Invites the moon to dance with the trees.
With fireflies glowing like stars in the night,
They spin and twirl, oh what a sight!

Laughter lingers in the calm air,
As crickets recite their songs without a care.
Sweet shadows play games in the dusk's warm glow,
Imbuing the night with a magical flow.

Dance of the Berry Spirits

A berry bash under the willow's sway,
Where the spirits gather, come join the fray.
With strawberry crowns and raspberry shoes,
They jiggle and wiggle, not one has the blues.

Cherries in tow, they whirl with delight,
As blueberries giggle in the soft moonlight.
The grass tickles toes, and the world seems to sway,
With each joyful twirl, they begin the ballet.

Pineapple hats and a grape for a nose,
Frolicsome frolics as their laughter grows.
From branch to branch, the joy spreads wide,
Who knew berry spirits could dance with such pride?

Each twinkling star joins in the fun,
As the forest watches, a thrill has begun.
In the dance of the fruits, life feels complete,
With laughter and music, oh, what a treat!

The Enchanted Orchard

In an orchard where the fruits all chuckle,
A pear wears a bowtie and starts to shuffle.
Grapes in sunglasses, looking so fine,
They sip on cool lemonade, feeling divine.

A rambunctious apple tells puns so sweet,
While peachy giggles tickle our feet.
With pom-poms made of leaves, they cheer,
For every little pun that we hear!

The trees sway to rhythm, a fruity parade,
Where the sunbeams come down in a bright cascade.
Nuts crack jokes while bees buzz in tune,
Under the watchful smile of the moon.

In this kooky orchard, every day's fun,
With a sprinkle of whimsy for everyone.
So join in the laughter, don't be shy,
In the enchanted orchard, let your worries fly.

The Heartbeat of Nature's Patchwork

In the garden where strawberries strut,
A squirrel debates if he'll wear a nut.
Daisies dance with tales to share,
While bees do ballet without a care.

The sun plays peek-a-boo with the shade,
As lost socks remind of laundry trade.
A rabbit hops like it's got a plan,
While ants argue who's the fastest man.

A wise old tree whispers in the breeze,
"Hey, grasshopper, don't forget to sneeze!"
Giggles erupt from a nearby stream,
As nature's patches join the dream.

With each chirp, a joke in the air,
The crickets tut their funny despair.
The heartbeat of color sings with glee,
Nature's patchwork, wild and free.

Enchanted Footsteps in the Wild

A fox in boots twirls and prances,
While mushrooms join in funny dances.
The wind tells stories with a tickle,
As pine trees laugh a playful chuckle.

Bumblebees buzz with a sass so grand,
Telling flowers, "You're bland, take a stand!"
A snail in shades crawls a path of gold,
Singing tales of adventures bold.

Underneath the mossy, soft embrace,
A frog prepares for a jump in place.
He leaps for joy, then splashes around,
"Now that's what I call a glorious sound!"

A chubby chipmunk tries to sing,
But all that comes out is a funny thing.
The wild wraps laughter in its wild art,
With enchanted footsteps, it wins the heart.

Soliloquy of the Forest Delights.

In the woods, a tree takes the stage,
Proclaiming softly its timeless age.
"If I could dance, I would shimmy and sway,
But roots hold me back, alas, I must stay!"

A squirrel with dreams of Broadway fame,
Practices lines like he's in the game.
With acorns as props, he strikes a pose,
The audience—mushrooms, they giggle, they doze.

The owls hoot out a nightly tune,
As fireflies twinkle like stars in June.
They host a show where the laughter ignites,
Soliloquies sung by glowing delights.

As night falls softly, with jokes in the air,
The nightingales sing without a care.
Nature abounds in its whims and frights,
In the soliloquy of forest delights.

Wild Vine Whispers

In tangled greens where secrets dwell,
A wild vine whispers, "Can you tell?
The daisies gossip, yet miss the clue,
As mushrooms noddle, 'Is that really true?'

Laughter rolls down the mossy hill,
While a hedge pig attempts to chill.
"Why take life serious?" chuckles the thyme,
"Let's twist and turn in nature's rhyme!"

Leaves rustle with hints of a silly play,
As beetles plot a grand getaway.
A playful chortle from the nearby brook,
Makes every turn a funny nook.

With every fold of the vine's embrace,
A secret shared, a light-hearted space.
The wild whispers tease, with joy they shine,
In the gentle jest of nature's design.

Berries at Dusk

At twilight's glow, the fruits are bright,
Flavors burst, oh what a sight!
A mischievous squirrel steals a treat,
Dancing shadows, oh what a feat!

The berries giggle in the breeze,
Tickled by whispers of the trees.
A rogue raccoon joins in the fun,
Chasing fireflies, one by one.

With juice-stained paws, they laugh aloud,
A fruity party, oh so proud!
Underneath the silver moon,
Nature's jesters sing a tune.

So gather round, both small and tall,
Join the laughter, come one, come all!
In berry patches, mirth unfolds,
Stories of sweetness yet untold.

Rhythms in the Untamed

In the wild woods, a jazzy beat,
Berries bounce to a funky seat.
Badgers tap their furry toes,
While berry bushes wear bright clothes.

The foxes prance with playful flair,
Wobbling like they just don't care.
A hedgehog spins, a breakdance whiff,
In nature's club, what a gift!

The mushrooms plop like drums on ground,
While dandelions sway, profound.
With giggles shared, both loud and short,
Nature's rhythm is quite the sport.

So shimmy under that leafy roof,
Let's bust a move, let's share our woof!
With every berry, laughter shines,
In the wild dance of twinkling vines.

The Wild Gardener's Tune

A gardener with a wild know-how,
Wears a hat that's too large now.
With spatula and trowel, they declare,
"Give me berries, I'll sow some flair!"

Plants go bouncing, seeds in flight,
Chasing butterflies in delight.
Gardening gnomes are in the mix,
Telling tales with every fix.

Dandelions pirouette with grace,
While weeds groove in a leafy race.
A chipmunk jests, a raccoon swoops,
In this garden of giggly fruits!

Laughter sprouts alongside the blooms,
As the wild tune of nature looms.
Long live the laughter, sweet and bright,
In this garden where joy takes flight!

An Ode to Nature's Bounty

Oh plump and juicy treasures found,
In vines and brambles, joy abounds.
The berries chuckle, sweet on the tongue,
As creatures dance and sing their song.

A frolicking rabbit makes its dash,
Sniffing out treats with a happy splash.
The worms do a wiggly, happy jig,
Rave parties held for every twig!

The sun dips low, the stars appear,
Frogs in the pond croak cheerily near.
With berries ripe, we raise a toast,
To the silly things that we love most!

So join the fun, both wild and free,
In nature's harvest jubilee.
For every berry, laugh we will,
In the bounty's glow, our hearts are still.

Nature's Unsung Harmonies

In the meadow, frogs sing loud,
With crickets chirping, they're so proud.
A cow may moo, a dog may bark,
In this symphony, they leave their mark.

Fluffy clouds drift, lazy and slow,
They take their time, just like a pro.
When wind chimes jingle, it's quite the spree,
Nature's band, oh, come and see!

Squirrels debate which tree is best,
While ants march on, they never rest.
Who knew the forest could be so sweet?
With all these tunes, it can't be beat!

A dance of leaves in the gentle breeze,
A playful moment that's sure to please.
So join the fun, come laugh and play,
Nature's chorus brightens the day!

Moss-Covered Melodies

Mossy carpets beneath our feet,
Where mouse may dance and hedgehogs meet.
Each step we take, a giggle grows,
The earth below has jokes, who knows?

Fungus friends in silly hats,
Giggling as they chat with bats.
Toadstools with spots, a painter's dream,
In this green world, we reign supreme!

A snore from rocks, a yawn from trees,
Nature chuckles in every breeze.
Covered in moss, they shake and sway,
Turning the dull into a play!

So come enjoy this woodland game,
Where laughter blooms and there's no shame.
In every nook, a melody thrives,
The forest sings, and joy survives!

A Tangle of Hues and Hues

Daisies twirl in dresses bright,
Sunflowers strut in golden light.
A patchwork quilt of colors grand,
A riot of shades in this fair land.

Ladybugs wearing polka dots,
Dance with bees sharing honey spots.
What a sight, a vibrant show,
In this wild gallery, spirits glow!

The rainbow puddles by the brook,
Where frogs jump in for a fun look.
Forget the gray, let's paint it true,
With stripes and splotches, a lively hue!

So let's all splash in the color spree,
Laughing 'neath the blooming tree.
In this tangle of hues, we'll play,
Creating joy with every ray!

Whimsy in the Briar's Embrace

Briar patches hold a secret flair,
Where mischievous critters often stare.
Rabbits' hats and hedgehogs' shoes,
In this playful world, you just can't lose.

Bumblebees wear tiny ties,
While butterflies float in the skies.
Everything here seems a bit askew,
With all this whimsy, how could it be blue?

Thorns may poke, but laughter flows,
With friends around, anything goes.
So join the fun in this tangled space,
Where joy is found in every place!

Let's roll and tumble through the bramble,
In nature's dance, we shout and ramble.
For in this embrace, we find the light,
A whimsical day, oh, what a sight!

Songs of the Hidden Grove

In the grove where shadows play,
Squirrels dance the night away.
Nuts and berries, oh what a feast,
Join the party, get your beast!

Whispers of leaves, giggles of trees,
Even the roots sway in the breeze.
Mushrooms giggle, wearing their hats,
Playing tricks on nearby cats.

A raccoon croons, oh what a sight,
Under stars that twinkle bright.
The owls hoot, a comic refrain,
While crickets laugh like they're insane!

In this place where laughter reigns,
Nature hums its fun campaigns.
So join the chorus, sing along,
In the grove, where we all belong!

Lurking Under Velvet Leaves

Beneath the leaves, a mystery stirs,
A hedgehog juggles, a swirl of furs.
With tiny paws that are quick and spry,
He flips those acorns to the sky!

The ladybugs, in polka dots,
Are having a dance, oh, they're such twots!
They turn and spin in a twirly way,
While the ants debate, which game to play.

A frog leaps in, with quite the splash,
Splattering leaves, oh what a crash!
The bugs all cheer, "Now that's just grand!"
As laughter ripples through the land.

With velvet leaves as their cozy stage,
Creatures of all sizes engage.
Join the laughter, don't be shy,
Under the leaves, let spirits fly!

Plumage in the Twilight

In twilight's glow, the colors blaze,
Birds in hats cause quite the craze.
They strut and boast with all their might,
As fireflies dance in the fading light.

A parrot sings a cheeky tune,
While owls roll their eyes, oh so immune.
"Who's got the style?" they hoot and cheer,
As feathers fly, oh, what a sphere!

With every flap, a little jest,
In this bird party, they're all the best.
The sun bids adieu, stars take their post,
And laughter lingers, they love it most!

So join the flock, don your own flair,
Twilight's magic, with laughter to share.
In plumage bright, we'll take our flight,
And giggle till morning, with sheer delight!

The Wild Fruit's Serenade

Under the sun where wild fruits grow,
Berries joke with a cheeky glow.
Strawberries boast, "I'm the sweetest treat!"
While raspberries giggle, "Let's not compete!"

Peaches parade, fluffy and round,
"I'm the juiciest!" they cheerfully sound.
Kiwi winks with a sly little grin,
"Just wait till you taste my fuzzy skin!"

In a fruit bowl, they all unite,
Sharing laughter, what a delight!
With every peel and every bite,
The wild ones sing through day and night.

So grab a fruit, and join the fun,
In this orchard, everyone's spun.
Nature's chorus, vibrant and sweet,
With every chomp, we dance to the beat!

Beneath the Thicket's Charm

Under bushes, creatures play,
Silly squirrels dance all day.
Hiding nuts without a care,
While the rabbits play truth or dare.

A fox attempts a daring leap,
Trips and falls, no need to weep.
The thicket laughs, a jolly sound,
As all the critters gather 'round.

A hedgehog rolls, a spiky ball,
Pokes the badger, that's his call.
"Let's race!" they say, then off they go,
In a tangled mess, fast and slow.

Beneath the thicket, life is bright,
With chuckles shared, pure delight.
Every twist and turn we find,
Leaves a giggle light behind.

Hummingbird's Ink and Nectar

A hummingbird sips divine,
Swirling colors, oh so fine.
Writing poems, quick and blink,
With a drop of sweetened ink.

Buzzing round from bloom to bloom,
Filling hearts with sweet perfume.
"Watch me dance!" it seems to sing,
While the flowers all take wing.

Wings a-whir, what a sight!
In the sun, they twinkle bright.
With a flick and a flap, they twist,
Creating joy, can't be missed.

All the bees join in the fun,
Sharing laughter, one by one.
In a flap and flutter spree,
Nectar spills with glee, whee!

Myths on Thorny Twists

In a maze of thorns so tight,
A tale's spun from day to night.
A rosy dragon, quite absurd,
Claims he's king, just look at him purr!

A wise old owl, full of tricks,
Says the thorns are part of the mix.
Tangled tales with laughter shared,
Hoots and giggles, magic's aired.

Wandering through the prickly paths,
Finding joy in witty laughs.
Foxes whisper tales so sly,
Of treasure chests that fly high.

Every twist a quirky plot,
A spider adds a swing and knot.
In the brambles, smiles abound,
With myths that tickle all around.

Echoes of the Hidden Hollow

In a hollow, giggles rise,
Bouncing off the secret skies.
Bunnies peek from grassy dens,
Playing tricks on all their friends.

A turtle tries to race the breeze,
But ends up snoozing 'neath the trees.
A lively quack from ducks nearby,
"Wake up slowpoke, come on! Fly!"

The echoes bounce with silly cheer,
As friends all gather, drawing near.
"Let's tell tales of joy and jest,
In our hollow, we are blessed!"

Through the bushes, laughter flows,
Hidden secrets, everyone knows.
In the cozy nook, we stay,
Sharing echoes day by day.

Patterns in the Tangle

In the bushes, where I peek,
A squirrel chases its own cheek.
Twisting, turning, oh what fun,
Be careful, or you'll be outrun!

Tangled branches wave so proud,
Whisper tales, both strange and loud.
Bees are buzzing, what's the buzz?
A leafy dance, oh yes it does!

Every thicket has a tale,
Of a raccoon with a wild tale.
Jumping, shouting, squirrels prance,
In the thorns, they seem to dance!

Nature's circus, full of cheer,
Juggling berries far and near.
In the muddle, life is grand,
Laughter echoes through the land!

Rhapsody of the Growing Green

In the garden, sprouts abound,
Tiny dancers on the ground.
Lettuce shares a leafy smile,
Tomatoes blush with juicy style.

Cucumbers whisper, 'Have a taste!'
While carrots hide, not in haste.
Peas are giggling, rolling free,
Underneath the bumblebee!

Wiggly worms below the soil,
Toiling hard without a toil.
Radishes giggle, red and round,
Making mischief underground!

Every seed, a tale to tell,
Of sun and rain, it grows so well.
When you walk through green delight,
Watch for critters, what a sight!

Fragrant Echoes in the Fog

In the morning mist, a brew,
Scents of berries—who knew?
Dewdrops sparkle, softly cling,
While birds break out in chirpy sing.

Lemons giggle in the haze,
Cinnamon rolls, they spin and blaze.
Flavors twirl through foggy air,
With each swirl, there's joy to share!

The peppermint winks, 'I'm so cool!'
While thyme's a jokester in this school.
Ginger snaps from off the shelf,
'Let's have fun, just be yourself!'

As the sun breaks through the grey,
Sweets and spices come to play.
In this fog of fragrant bliss,
Don't forget to steal a kiss!

Hidden Paths of the Orchard

Whispers float from bough to bough,
Where apples grin and trees take bows.
A pear is blushing, what a sight,
Underneath the golden light.

The paths are twisted, winding slow,
Where curious critters come and go.
Pigs in costumes, oh so proud,
They strut their stuff, they're quite the crowd!

Cherries play peek-a-boo with bees,
While dancing leaves hang from the trees.
Every corner hides a treat,
In this orchard, life's so sweet!

Weave through shadows, secrets unfold,
With whimsical tales, the trees foretold.
In every twist, a giggle waits,
Join the dance, oh don't be late!

Dreams Among Berry-Laden Boughs

In the garden where the berries grow,
A squirrel named Sam puts on a show.
He tiptoes under the blueberry jam,
And sings to the moon like a very weird lamb.

The cherries giggle as he trips on a root,
A dance with the daisies, oh what a hoot!
With each berry pluck, a new joke is hatched,
Even the fledglings are happilymatched.

The blackberries tease with poky allure,
As Sam makes a face that's quite hard to endure.
He dreams of a pie that is big as a house,
While dodging a thicket and a sneaky mouse.

So here's to the fun beneath foliage tight,
Where laughter and berries are pure delight.
In the dreams of that garden, we all can rejoice,
Just listen to Sam and his jolly old voice.

Thicket's Chronicle

Amid the tangled stems and vines galore,
Lived a hedgehog named Henry with tales to explore.
He'd recount his adventures with berries so sweet,
While balancing boxes of jam on his feet.

One day he tripped and rolled down a slope,
As a rabbit named Rob found it hard to cope.
With a flop and a flop, they both laughed in glee,
Beneath the bright branches of a nut-laden tree.

The elderberry crew joined in on the fun,
Creating a ruckus beneath the warm sun.
There were chortles and snorts as they filled up their hats,

With every wild tale that came from the fats.

In the heart of the thicket, where shenanigans bloom,
Life spins like a blueberry pie from the womb.
And Henry the hedgehog with stories, no doubt,
Keeps our giggles alive—there's never a drought!

Where Wild Things Whisper

In a field where the wild things softly croon,
Lived a fox and a bear who danced 'neath the moon.
They'd play hide and seek in the raspberry hedge,
And laugh at the wind as it grabbed at their edge.

The bear tried to jive, but his feet went a-flop,
While the fox in his scarf continued to hop.
With a splash of the berries, colors took flight,
Their whispers grew louder as day turned to night.

But a snippy old crow swooped in for some fun,
And cackled, "You creatures are outdone, just run!"
With a wiggle and jiggle, they danced on their toes,
Leaving trails of sweet laughter wherever she goes.

So in this wild spot, where the critters all play,
The whispers and giggles will never decay.
Join the fox and the bear in their ballet of dreams,
Where fun takes the stage and it endlessly beams.

Delights of the Hidden Path

Down a lane that twirls with a magical twist,
A hedgehog named Hector makes quite the list.
He ventures where mushrooms sprout hats of delight,
And chuckles at hedges that tickle the night.

With a basket of laughter and a dollop of cheer,
He finds silly things that just might disappear.
A porcupine giggles as he rolls in the mud,
While the berries all cheer, "Let's dance in the flood!"

The path splits and twirls, like a dancer's grand spin,
As Hector discovers the magic within.
While the fireflies twinkle with mischief and glee,
He shoos them away yelling, "No light's for me!"

So wander the lane where the curious dwell,
With Hector, the hedgehog, who knows it so well.
Dig in to the laughter, let silliness reign,
In the delights of the hidden path, joy is gained!

Berry Moonlit Soliloquies

Under the moon, the berries giggle,
Dancing shadows, hear them wiggle.
A squirrel in a cap, pondering his fate,
Thinks he's a chef, but can't find the plate.

With fluffy clouds, they paint the scene,
Joking with stars, so bright and keen.
The critters gather, for a midnight snack,
But end up with jam, and a blueberry smack.

Chirping crickets join the play,
Telling tales of berries, come what may.
In the back, a beetle does a jig,
While ants complain, "That's too big!"

So raise a glass to midnight cheer,
Where laughter bubbles, far and near.
For in this grove, humor's the king,
And all together, we joyfully sing.

Where the Rich Soil Breathes

In fields where laughter blooms so bright,
The soil exclaims, 'What pure delight!'
A worm writes poetry, soft and slow,
While daisies argue, 'I'm the star of the show!'

Sunshine beams with a cheeky grin,
As bumblebees buzz, their tales begin.
A rabbit hops dressed in a coat,
Swears he's the finest, take note, take note!

The puddles giggle when raindrops fall,
'Look who's here, the rain has a ball!'
Foxes play tag, the fun never ends,
In this muddy chaos, every creature blends.

So come join the dance, it's wild and free,
In the rich soil where joy is a spree.
With nature's humor shaping the land,
Let's laugh together, hand in hand.

Bottled Rainbows of the Meadow

In the meadow, colors collide,
With petals and leaves, they take a ride.
A butterfly sneezes, oh what a sight!
Sprinkling hues, making day turn bright.

The sunflowers gossip, sharing their tales,
Telling of bees and their clumsy fails.
A ladybug spins, in splendid delight,
Wearing a vest, oh what a fright!

Grasshoppers leap with style and flair,
Telling the daisies, 'How do we fare?'
While tulips sway, in a rhythmic lineup,
A bunny sits back, sipping from a cup.

So let's toast to this colorful crew,
In bottled rainbows, the laughter grew.
For in this meadow, where colors play,
The funny antics make bright every day.

A Tidal Poem of Color and Life

At the shore where colors blend and clash,
The sand crabs dance, in a funky flash.
Seagulls squawk in a comical way,
As they steal fries—'Hey, not today!'

Waves giggle softly, teasing the beach,
Painting the sand, just out of reach.
A fish in a bow tie dreams of the sky,
While jellyfish float, feeling quite spry.

The sandcastle's king wears a crown made of shells,
Ruling the beach, where laughter swells.
Starfish gather, for a silly debate,
Who's best at fishing, or dancing with fate?

So splash in the water, feel the delight,
In this tidal poem, life is bright.
Where each wave brings a chuckle anew,
And the color of laughter shines through and through.

Thorn-kissed Serenade

In the thicket where shadows play,
Thorns giggle and dance in sway.
Berries whisper secrets near,
Poking fun, they spread good cheer.

A bird swoops low, checks its flight,
Dodging brambles, what a sight!
Fruits seem to chuckle in glee,
Nature's jesters, wild and free.

A sassy squirrel with fuzzy paws,
Mocks the thorns without a cause.
He snickers as he dashes past,
A thorny joke that's unsurpassed!

Underneath the vines' embrace,
Laughter blooms in every space.
Who knew that prickles could be fun?
A serenade for everyone!

Secrets Beneath the Bramble

Hidden secrets, oh what a tease,
Underneath the leaves and trees.
A rabbit whispers tales of gold,
While tangled vines are bold and old.

A sneaky fox with a grin so wide,
Peeks through branches with bated pride.
"Hey there!" he calls with cheeky glee,
"What's your secret? Share it with me!"

The thorns respond with rustling sounds,
"Hush! The berries talk, not hounds!"
A mischievous crow caws near,
Plucking berries without fear.

As laughter bounces off each wall,
A chorus of secrets, one and all.
Beneath the bramble, tales unwind,
A funny treasure for us to find!

Berry-laden Twilight

At twilight's kiss, the berries glow,
Tickling twilight with a show.
A hedgehog waltzes with a flair,
While berries roll without a care.

Fireflies giggle, lighting the way,
As they join the jokes in playful sway.
"Hey there, fruit!" they dance around,
A berry bash in playful sound!

The little mushrooms join the fun,
Cap to cap, they hop and run.
"Why so serious?" one does say,
When all around is a berry ballet!

With chuckles shared in purple light,
The creatures play 'til the end of night.
In the bramble, under starry dome,
Berry-laden laughter calls us home!

The Poetry of Wild Harvest

In fields where wild things grow and sing,
The berry harvest starts to fling.
Nature's poets with a pun or two,
Compose verses, fresh and new.

"Hurry up!" the elderberry shouts,
"Join the fun! Let's see who scouts!"
Raspberries giggle as they're plucked,
With every twist, a rhyme is tucked.

The young ones tumble in wild zest,
Rolling in fruit, they feel the best.
"Oh, don't mind us!" they cheer and play,
Making memories on berry day.

So raise a glass to the fruity cheer,
With laughter ringing loud and clear.
In the wild's feast, we all partake,
The poetry of harvest, make no mistake!

Garden of Spectral Melodies

In a garden where shadows dance,
A squirrel tries his luck with a glance,
Cartwheeling daisies, a mischievous charm,
While roses plot tricks with a droning alarm.

The carrots wear hats, quite a sight,
Radishes giggle with all of their might,
Sunflowers whisper, their petals are bright,
Chasing the clouds in a playful flight.

Twirling in circles, the peas sing out loud,
In this garden, mischief draws quite a crowd,
With beetles in bowties and ladybugs bold,
They're writing the story that never gets old.

So join in the fun where the weird things play,
Magic abounds in a curious way,
Under the moon, with its mischievous gleam,
The garden awakens, alive with a dream.

Rhapsody of the Untamed

A raccoon in a tux, oh what a surprise,
Dancing atop the fence, under wide-open skies,
He twirls and he spins, with a wink of his eye,
While crickets keep time, their chorus will fly.

The owls share the stage, in monocles round,
With voices like velvet, they're quite astound,
Bouncing on mushrooms that bounce just the same,
The night's a big party, and all are in game.

The fireflies flash, a strobe in the night,
While frogs leap around, with their splendid delight,
They croak in a rhythm, and soon they'll invite,
A chorus of laughter till morning's first light.

So gather your friends, let the wild things roam,
From under the stars, let the fun find a home,
In this symphony bright, where chaos looks grand,
The untamed are kings in this vibrant land.

Fable of the Pastry Skipper

There once was a chef, with floury hands,
Who danced with the pastries, in floury bands,
With cookies for shoes and pies for a hat,
He'd twirl through the kitchen, oh fancy that!

A croissant did laugh, with a buttery grin,
While tarts threw confetti, let the fun begin,
They juggled their fruits, a spectacular sight,
As the whisk took a bow, with great morning light.

The muffins wore capes, flying high in the air,
Whilst macarons stood, with a silky glare,
A battle of sweetness, oh what a delight,
A sugar-filled fable, that lasted all night.

So when you bake treats, don't forget to embrace,
The magic that happens when sweets take their place,
For in every dough, and each sprinkle's cheer,
Lies the story of laughter, that's utterly clear.

Layers of Sunshine and Gloom

In a land of bright socks and mismatched shoes,
The clouds like popcorn forgot their muse,
Sunshine and rainbows, they spar and they play,
While shadows roll in without much delay.

The cacti wear smiles, with prickles that beam,
And giggling in corners, the mushrooms all scream,
With toadstools in tuxes, and daisies in line,
In this quirky parade, odd is perfectly fine.

A cat in a bowtie pens poems of fate,
While puddles reflect the joy at a rate,
The sun hugs the moon, as they struggle to meet,
In a world woven odd, where oddness is sweet.

So frolic alongside the whimsy in gloom,
Encouraging laughter wherever you zoom,
For in each silly twist, a giggle will bloom,
In the layers of life, where joy finds its room.

Nightfall in the Berry Thicket

As night descends on tangled vines,
The critters dance in berry lines.
Silly squirrels in hats so bright,
Share secrets 'neath the pale moonlight.

A wise old owl hoots out a jest,
While fireflies put on their best dress.
The thicket buzzes with laughter clear,
As berries giggle, full of cheer.

Butterflies and Bramble Tales

Butterflies flitter with stories grand,
Of kites and mushrooms that dance on land.
While brambles whisper a tuneful song,
As the day's antics stretch all night long.

A beetle in specs reads poetry loud,
While the daisies giggle, all feeling proud.
In this field of wonders so wild and free,
Every corner holds a tale, just wait and see!

Glimmers of Dawn on Silent Trails

Dawn peeks in with a yawn and a stretch,
Beneath the dew, silly shadows fetch.
The berries blush with the new day's light,
Ready to play in the morning's sight.

Twirling rabbits in a berry race,
With laughter that quickens their little pace.
The sun's a jester with beams so bright,
Tickling the thicket till it's full of delight.

The Secret Life of Berries

In hidden nooks, the berries scheme,
Plotting mischief like a wild dream.
They wear tiny crowns made of dew,
Planning a party for me and you.

When the moon comes out, they jump and jive,
Bouncing to tunes where the critters thrive.
With giggles and cheer, they steal the show,
Life's a berry blast, as all friends know.

www.ingramcontent.com/pod-product-compliance
Lightning Source LLC
Chambersburg PA
CBHW070750220426
43209CB00083B/358